# Oxford at Night

Photographs by Norman McBeath

Photographs by Norman McBeath

Introduction by Jeanette Winterson

# Oxford at Night

Easel Press  2006

FOR SARAH SMITH

Published by Easel Press on the occasion of the exhibition
Oxford at Night: Photographs by Norman McBeath held at
The Ashmolean Museum, Oxford, 9 May to 23 July 2006.

Easel Press · 4 Learmonth Gardens Mews · Edinburgh EH4 1EX

ISBN 0-9552859-0-9 / 978-0-9552859-0-5

Designed and typeset by Dalrymple
Printed and bound in Italy by Conti Tipicolor, Florence

Front cover: Bodleian Library and Sheldonian Theatre
Back cover: Corpus Christi College
Opposite title page: Pembroke College

It is as though we were walking swiftly through the night, when suddenly we round a corner into an empty space. We slow down, look up at the lighted windows, into the darkened doorway. The air is clean with stars and we are alone.

But we are not alone because this silent watching space is the walls against our hands and the stones under our feet. Do we dream it or does it dream us?

I have lived with these photographs in my studio for months. Over time I have come to understand that they are studies of the Oxford I know, and openings into an Oxford that may or may not exist.

At first the photographs feel familiar; railings, columns, stonework, paving, door cases, bollards, bicycles. Here is the Oxford that ties itself into time, and is anchored to its architecture.

Oxford is recognisable all over the world. It is a brand as well as an institution. Its appeal is its ability to fuse the past with the present. It can be inhabited at many levels, even when the visitor only recognises this sub-consciously. Of course it is beautiful, but it is also continuous. Oxford is a museum, in that it houses the past, but it is also a living city that homes the present. It is elegant and iconic, but it is real, too.

These photographs capture the structured beauty of Oxford, but without cliché. This is not picture-postcard Oxford. The still emptiness of each frame questions us about where we are, and why we have come here. Who else is here too? No one that we can see, but there are lives behind the lighted windows, and footsteps, surely, just ahead of us in the night?

The realism of the photographs – the undoubted and described nature of Oxford, jostles with their surreal quality. Lewis Carroll understood

Oxford's doubleness when he wrote *Alice in Wonderland*. This is a city, like Venice, where there is more than one reality; what lies on the surface leads to something stranger.

When I look at these photographs, I am haunted by what is offered beyond, or through their surface. The long, well-known streets could lead anywhere. The darkened door case conceals who knows what? Even the bicycles, ubiquitous and ordinary, take on a different meaning when abandoned in tangled piles, or left single and solitary under a lamp-post.

Night changes everything. The shadows and shapes of the night cast the day into its negative. The photographs here have become their own negatives, dark and elusive, asking that we develop them further, by entering their world. Night is the opposite of the busy day, where action rules the moment. Night is more secretive and contemplative and does not give up its meaning as easily as the daylight hours. There is a collusion. We are invited but we choose to enter. Daytime is inevitable; *we must*. Night-time is complicity; *we choose*.

As we walk into the night-world of the photographs, the Oxford we know is just behind us, and the unmarked city is beginning. There are no signs, no directions. There are known objects, yes, but these are not coordinates, these are challenges. We will have to read them as runes. We will have to feel our way across the stonework, trust that the paving is solid, hope that the bicycle is unlocked. We might need to get away quickly. We might need to find a way back.

The geometric reassurance of the photographs is a disguise. The planes and angles, cubes and masses, should not deceive us into believing that this is a secure place. The shadows are the clue – the buildings are only shadows of shadows. In the night-world, the darkness is real; what appears out of the darkness should not be depended upon. It may disappear. It may be a mirage. The solid world of objects gives way to a world of images; empty space and points of light.

The structure of the atom; empty space and points of light. The atomic truth of our existence is best understood at night. We are not solid; we are wavering, changing, multiple. The reassurance of objects is an illusion. At night, it is possible to see further than daylight allows, and the photographs here use the night-light to uncover truths missing in the day.

These dark angels, like all angels, are messengers and guides. We will not be led to anywhere we know already – that is not the business of angels, and we may sense other presences that make us uncomfortable. To live fully in the known is to *unknow* it, as St Teresa of Avila, and William Blake understood, or as T. S. Eliot put it, 'to know the place for the first time'. This wonder and revelation is only possible if for a while, we are blind-folded and spun round, as in a children's game, and then let loose to see the world again.

Art is a way of letting this happen – the strangeness, disorientation, newness. We need art because we need to look, and look again, as though we had never seen it before, which is usually in the gift of the artist to give, and us to find, and give back.

The next time you walk through Oxford at night, walk through it twice; once in the world you know, and once in the world just revealing itself to you.

1  Clarendon Building

2 Bridge of Sighs

3 Radcliffe Square

4 Oriel Square

6 Merton Street

7 Corpus Christi College

9 Radcliffe Camera

11 Corpus Christi College

12  St. Mary's Passage

15 Catte Street

17 Jesus College Chapel

19 The Turl

Norman McBeath is an independent photographer whose work focuses on people and places. The National Portrait Galleries in London and Edinburgh have a number of his portraits in their permanent collections. His exhibition 'Beyond Beirut', commissioned by the British Council, was shown in London, the Middle East and North Africa. Recent work has been exhibited at the Leica Gallery in New York, Edinburgh Printmakers and the Royal Scottish Academy. Having been based in Oxford for many years he now lives in Edinburgh.

www.normanmcbeath.com

Jeanette Winterson won the Whitbread Prize for Best First Novel for *Oranges Are Not the Only Fruit*. Since then she has published seven other novels including *The Passion*, *Written on the Body* and *The PowerBook*, a collection of short stories, *The World and Other Places*, a book of essays, *Art Objects*, *Lighthousekeeping* and a children's picture book, *The King of Capri*. Her most recent piece of adult fiction is *Weight*, a retelling of the Atlas myth for Canongate's Myth series. She has adapted her work for TV, film and stage. Her books are published in thirty-two countries and this year she was awarded the OBE for services to literature. She lives in Oxfordshire and London.

www.jeanettewinterson.com

Acknowledgements Very special thanks are due to Jeanette Winterson for agreeing to write the introduction, producing such an original and imaginative response to these photographs. Thanks are also due to Timothy Wilson, Keeper of Western Art, at the Ashmolean Museum for organizing the exhibition and for helping with the costs involved. Also to Susie Gault, Bridget Allen, Geraldine Glynn and Alan Kitchen at the Ashmolean Museum for their invaluable support throughout the preparations.